Dreamer

A Collection of Poems and Dreams

Terri Skuce

First printing, 2014
Printed in the United States of America

ISBN-13: 978-1502799098
ISBN-10: 150279909X

Printed by CreateSpace, An Amazon.com Company

Available from Amazon.com, CreateSpace.com,
and other retail outlets

For additional information, please visit
www.terrafirmapress.com

This book is dedicated with love and gratitude to my husband and son.

CONTENTS

For Specific People

Various Forms

Introduction

For as long as I can remember, I've had a fascination with dreams - my own and the dreams of other people. I enjoy hearing and musing about them, as well as discussing them.

Whenever I can remember my dreams, I like to examine them for any lessons they might contain. I believe our dreams can speak to us of what is in our souls... what we fear and wrestle with, what excites or soothes us, and what our desires and disappointments are. They can draw our attention to things in our lives that we might want to deal with or change.

I'm still learning the language of my dreams, still attempting to understand the symbolism in them and looking to see if there are any messages to uncover. Of course, there are also times when I don't even try to make sense of what seems to be just pure enjoyment or intriguing nonsense.

My poetry comes from a dreamy place. It's not unusual for a fragment of a poem to pop into my head when I'm just drifting off to sleep. I keep a notebook beside my bed so I can jot those words or ideas down to be looked at some other time. I've learned that if I don't write these things down, they might be lost forever.

Other pieces of poems appear when I'm daydreaming. I hear two lines in my head and think *"What a wonderful idea!"* and I rush to write them down. Sometimes, I take those two lines and a cup of coffee out to a comfortable corner of my garden. I sit and sip my coffee while waiting to see if the rest of the poem will appear. As I wait, I drink in the beauty of creation and feel a deep sense of gratitude for everything around me.

At other times, I fight to gain control of a poem. I struggle to capture it and mold it into lines on paper. Sometimes it gives up and submits to being shaped and developed, other times it doesn't. I have many, many poem bits that I've lost the battle with - all in a file folder waiting for that day when they might give up their secrets and allow me to write them down. Perhaps they'll be in a future book.

Some of my poems have come from personal experiences and others from imagining what an event or experience might be like for someone else. They all come from my own unique perspective which many people seem able to identify with.

I enjoy writing and have always known that I have a few books inside me somewhere. I just didn't dream that my first book would be a collection of poems. Over the years, many people have encouraged me to share my poems with others. So I have gathered them together in this book. Along with the poems, I have included two dreams that have significantly affected my life. They are the kind of dreams I enjoy hearing about and I am happy to share them with you.

Enjoy!

Terri

Welcome fellow dreamers.
Come dream with me a while;
partake of dreams 'til now untold
and share a tear or smile.

A Meaningful Dream

As I had often done in the recent days since my cancer diagnosis and treatment, I lay on my bed staring at the white stippled ceiling.

Oblivious to the sounds of my husband playing with our two-year-old son in the living room down the hall and the warm, golden afternoon sun streaming through the window, I was only aware of how I was feeling inside. Now that I was beginning to emerge from a heavy, gray fog of numbness that had wrapped itself around me every waking hour of each day for weeks, I felt a deep emotional pain.

On this memorable afternoon, I was trying to make sense of what had happened to me. Being a young woman, I had no frame of reference for such an unexpected, serious life event. I had no idea how to deal with what had happened to me. I only knew that my life had been irrevocably altered. Unable to turn back the clock to the time B.C. - Before Cancer - I knew that I had to somehow figure out how to incorporate this experience into the fibre of my being and discover who I now was.

I lay on my bed looking for answers. I stared at the ceiling asking myself what I would do with the remainder of my life if I knew that I had only two years left to live. My frustration at being unable to come up with any meaningful answers led to a feeling of desperation. I beseeched God to provide answers for me. "Please God, I need to know... what is the meaning of life anyhow?! Please, please tell me!"

I fell into a deep sleep and began to dream.

***

In my dream, I was taken by a guide of some sort to a place far away. I cannot describe the guide except to say that he had a male presence and seemed to be just a bit taller and somewhat older than I was. He communicated sparingly without words. I had a feeling of having thoughts, ideas and pictures placed into my mind. I was not afraid and I didn't question why he had come for me or where we were going.

We travelled what felt like quite a distance through a blank grayness. It seemed to me that we were flying yet there was no physical sensation of doing so. We arrived at a large building and walked through the main entrance. I saw that there were many rooms in this vast place. We went down a long, empty hallway of doors. At the end of the hallway, we entered a door that opened into a very large room.

I was struck by the incredible beauty of the room. It was like an old-fashioned library in the home of a very wealthy person. Everything about the room was rich, warm and inviting. There were thick, deep, patterned carpets on the floor, large comfortable-looking leather chairs, walls trimmed with thick, dark, gleaming wood and full bookcases lining the walls - all lit by a rich, soft, warm glow.

As my eyes drank in the wondrous beauty of this place, my guide told me that all knowledge was in this room - knowledge about everything and everyone was here. I was excited by that thought and enthusiastic to learn more. I didn't know where to start. I wondered what questions I should ask... what things I should try to learn. I stood scanning the room for a cabinet that might hold drawers of cards that listed the books. My search was interrupted when I was told that everything about me and my life was also here in this room. That caught my attention! It caused me to feel a bit nervous and hesitant. Yet I was also curious about this and so, thinking I could investigate other knowledge later, I agreed to be shown things about myself.

A screen appeared around the room... like one of those 360-degree screens where you can see a marching band coming toward you, splitting apart in the middle and filing past you on both sides. Then behind you, you can see the back of the band as they continue on their way.

On the screen, images began to appear - images from my life. Standing beside my guide and watching the screen I soon realized that I was viewing times in my past when I had interacted with people and, by my words or actions, had caused them pain. I knew this because I was experiencing the emotions of those people on the screen. As scene after scene was shown, I felt overwhelmed by the depth of the emotional pain that I was being subjected to - the pain that I had caused others. I wished that I could somehow undo that. I watched and cried. I felt deep sorrow. Gradually, I ended up crumpled on the floor clutching my stomach and crying in pain, devastated by the things I had done and the words I had said.

My guide reached down and helped me to my feet, gently directing me to continue watching the screen. The scenes changed. They became times when I had interacted with people and brought light, love and life to their day. Again, I experienced the emotions of those people. I watched in awe as scene after scene played out. I saw so many things that I had forgotten. It seemed that there were countless times when I had made a difference in someone's life without realizing it. A lot of the actions I saw seemed so insignificant to me and yet I could see - and feel - that my actions had a positive impact. This left me feeling peaceful, calm and very grateful.

Eventually, the images on the screen disappeared. I turned to my guide and wanted to know more. His response was that more wasn't available to me. I had been shown all that I needed to see.

My guide led me out of the room, down the long hallway and out of the building.

***

I awoke with the strange feeling that sometimes occurs after a dream - the feeling that it had all been very real. It was such an unusual and intense experience. I went over and over it in my mind trying to understand what it all meant. It didn't take long for me to come to the conclusion that my question had been answered... the question I asked before falling asleep... "What is the meaning of life?"

The answer I came to is that the meaning of life is found in our relationships - in how we interact with people - and that it is important to be sensitive to the effects our actions and words might have on the lives of others.

Since that dream twenty-six years ago, many scenes have been added to that room full of knowledge. I regret that many additional painful scenes have been stored there over the years, yet I know that room also holds an abundance of positive interactions.

I have taken this dream lesson to heart and it has changed my life. I came to realize that, in this imperfect world we live in, regardless of how much I don't like it, there are times when causing pain is inevitable. I prefer to be kind, compassionate and loving and I find awareness is helpful with that. One of my greatest desires is to store many, many more positive scenes in that room.

Through the Years

Let's Dream

Let's dream of a coming day
where the dawn's golden light
    invites eyes to open clearly
and lips to smile warmly
    upon the waiting hours;

where the morning shower
    scrubs away the mud of yesterday
and cascades a prayer of hope
    into our souls;

where we walk into a workplace
    with a spring in our steps
ready to skip through and around
    the problems and pitfalls
that might be hiding in wait to trip us up;

where families and friends
    laugh and banter over food
that feeds the connections
    of hearts and souls
in a way that banishes
    loneliness and isolation.

Let's dream of living in a world
where love flows
    with the power of Niagara Falls,
where peace floats
    in the misty air we breathe
and gratitude is exhaled
    into every corner of our lives;
where contentment feels
    as soft as the top of an infant's fuzzy head,

and acceptance tastes as smooth and delicious
    as an ice cream cone on a hot day.

Let's dream that we are the heroes
    of our bedtime stories,
that the end of the day
    slips peacefully and easily into slumber
where we ride our dreams into tomorrow....

The Gift of a New Year

When enough time has passed by
    and experiences been lived
you come to understand
    that you are not alone unless you abandon yourself;
and all your thinking and feeling and doing
    influence how you perceive this life you live -
        this life that's touching others.

You come to understand
    that pain is a teacher and laughter is a cure
        and you'll live them again and again;
that mistakes are paving stones on the road you travel
    where stepping on a crack
        can't break anybody's back;
and the best rewards are in the journey
    where you never arrive.

So you live in a resilient softer skin,
out of your eyes
    you see what's in your altered soul,
out of your heart
    you share love,
out of your mouth
    flows kindness and encouragement,
in your nature
    rests patience and gratitude,
and you begin to feel like you're making progress
    as into the gift of a new year comes hope.

You'd Know

If you could hear my heart you'd know
it sings a song for you -
a steady rhythm pulsing out
with love that's strong and true.

If you could read my thoughts you'd know
I'm keeping you in mind.
To think of you when you're not here
is comforting I find.

If you could stroke my skin you'd know
it's craving for your touch.
No other person's gentle hand
can satisfy as much.

If you could smell the air you'd know
scent lingers when you leave.
Your odour's in the room with me,
more so than you'd believe.

If you could taste my tears you'd know
how many I have cried.
I'm left with only memories
now that you've gone and died.

This Day

It's early morning when I wake
and put the coffee on.
I gaze upon the rustic lake
and praise the coming dawn.

The sun comes up a golden hue
shines bright above the trees,
and all feels right this coming day
as birdsong fills the breeze.

The sun climbs higher in the sky
caressing on my skin,
it seeps into my waiting heart
and spreads its warmth within.

This day is made for gratitude,
for loving thoughts and peace,
for living well in moments filled
with joy that doesn't cease.

My Pathways

Every once in a while
my mind goes for a wander
down the pathways of my childhood.

I travel the dusty uneven stones
of all different sizes and shapes
placed in the ground by my own little hands,
experience by experience,
often struggling, a long time ago.

Some of these paths go in circles
around lakes where graceful swans glide
through the tears that were shed,
over joys and sorrows
when emotions just couldn't be contained.

Other pathways are dead ends.
One leads to a park where I played with friends
climbing on, over and under the bars,
twirling in dizzy delight on the swings
and thumping my rump on the teeter-totter.

Another goes to a childhood home.
Out front on the cracked sidewalk
is a hopscotch drawn in chalk.
In the yard, a wise old owl watches me
from the tree that I wasn't supposed to climb.

Far off in the distance
are snow-covered mountains,
beautiful against the blue sky,
old volcanoes gone dormant -
majestic and silent, guarding the landscape.

As I wander, I see many things and places.
I see where I came from.
I see where I went right
and where I went wrong.
I see where I haven't quite figured things out.

Every once in a while I stop;
I stop to ponder and consider.
I stop to readjust a broken or uneven stone
so that I don't trip or fall
on my next trek this way.

Smokey

I consider it a pity
that this pretty little kitty
does not appear to have a home
and so all she can do is roam
in search of someone with a treat
and that's how she finds food to eat.

I never know when she'll appear
and love it when she shows up here.
I offer her a turkey slice
although I know it won't suffice
but hope it keeps her going strong
when time between her meals is long.

She gobbles up the treat with haste
and not a speck can go to waste.
When done, she settles in a chair
to spend time grooming with great care.
I watch her with a loving smile.
Then we just visit for a while.

I look into her eyes of gold
and see a little heart so bold;
I scratch her chin and stroke her fur
to hear her lovely rumbling purr
and then I let her out the door
with hope that she'll come back once more.

Smokey is a little stray cat that wandered all around the Oakwater Resort where we stayed in Kissimmee, Florida in February 2014. She was named 'Smokey' by Linda, a family member who was also vacationing in Oakwater. Linda asked about Smokey at the resort office and was told that the cat didn't have a home, had been hanging around, and they didn't want people feeding her as they were hoping she'd disappear.

Smokey was about the size of a six-month-old kitten. She was very soft and personable. If she saw a person who fed her, she'd come running with a sweet meow. The first time she showed up, she appeared to be starving. I gave her two turkey slices and then put her out the lanai door. She climbed the screen trying to get back in. As her visits went by, she appeared less hungry - and even turned her nose up at a piece of bologna.

I was concerned for Smokey. She was so sweet and my heart went out to her. I wanted a loving home for her. I asked other visiting family members to take Smokey home with them - but they already had cats. I would have brought her home with me but it would have been difficult to bring her across the border.

At the end of February, just before we left Florida for home, I heard from Linda that one of the pool maintenance men had adopted Smokey. He had asked Linda to catch her for him. He told Linda that he would take Smokey to the vet to see if she had a microchip and, if she didn't, he and his wife would adopt her - which they did. I was so pleased that the story of Smokey had a happy ending.

Where's the Spring?

It's springtime in the capital
and all I see is snow.
Dear weatherman you got it wrong;
it should be green you know!

There should be sun and daffodils
and buds upon the trees.
Why don't I see the robins yet,
or butterflies or bees?

Oh ya, that's right, I just forgot...
I guess *I've* got it wrong.
I'm living in Ontario
where winter lasts too long!

The Captain

I sailed a boat of sorrow
upon a sea of tears
and there I was a long way out
alone and lost for years.

And no one came to save me
or if they even tried
I wouldn't recognize attempts
as something in me died.

The days were dark and dreary,
the sky held heavy rain,
and all of it was lost on me
in unrelenting pain.

I saw boats in the distance,
just specks upon the sea,
they seemed too far to try to reach -
I had no energy.

Eventually I struggled
to help myself a bit.
Although I almost gave up hope
I didn't want to quit.

I started feeling angry
at everything and more.
I didn't want to be this way
but couldn't find the shore.

I shouted to the heavens
"Release me from this hell!"
and if my cry was heard by God
I really couldn't tell.

I bargained with my Maker...
if He'd reverse my plight
then I'd do everything I could
and do it all just right.

I waited for His answer
and saw no change in fate.
Despair and sadness gnawed at me
with their internal hate.

I languished on that ocean
a long time just obsessed
without the will to seek relief
from being so depressed.

And all I did was lie there
amid my misery,
blind and deaf and numb to life,
with not a hope or plea.

I let the sea waves lull me;
they tossed me to and fro.
There didn't seem to be a way
to fight against my woe.

And as I lay there resting
I slowly was restored.
I started to accept what was
and life was my reward!

So then the clouds were parted.
The sun came out to shine.
I saw the other boats out there,
some sailing close to mine.

I hailed a nearby captain
and asked which way to go.
That fellow had been here before
and so he seemed to know.

He beckoned me to follow.
I slowly made my way.
He led me to where I could see
the land I'm on today.

I set my sail and headed
toward that welcome land,
relieved at having someone come
and offer me a hand.

I turned back to that captain
to shout my thanks again
and saw that he was heading back
to rescue other men.

I Run

I run each second morning.
I run to clear my mind.
I run because I want to
tighten up my soft behind.

I run when it is sunny,
in shorts to tan my skin.
I run because I want to
see my body getting thin.

I run to ease my worries,
to have a life that's long.
I run because I want to
feel my muscles getting strong.

I run because I'm aging,
my birthday is in June.
I run because I want to
and I'm turning fifty soon.

I run for health and wellness,
to help myself feel good.
I run because I want to
and I think I darn-well should.

I tell myself I want to
but really know instead...
I run but I don't want to
'cause I'd rather stay in bed!

Time to Break Up

I cannot bear your neediness,
the way you speak my name,
misperceptions and assumptions -
you thinking we're the same.

You're too judgemental and aloof,
don't listen very well,
and so lacking in awareness
to be with you is hell.

I just don't have the tolerance
for all these things you do;
I feel driven to distraction -
It isn't me, it's you.

That you feel you are a victim
is very evident.
I wonder if it's possible
for you to feel content.

I feel for you, I really do
but that is not enough
for me to want to hang around
and put up with your stuff.

These things have gone on far too long.
It's time to set you free.
I'll tell you how I really feel -
it isn't you, it's me.

Sparkling Facets

We are like gemstones,
multifaceted jewels in hiding -
there to be discovered by those who would search.

Brought to light, our facets sparkle,
depending on the setting -
and the time and effort taken to discover them all.

The Rose

My heart is in this garden.
This garden's in my heart.
Toil and tears and great delight
are found in every part.

You were in my heart once, too -
and you gave me a rose.
Even though the love is gone,
I tend it and it grows.

The memories have faded
but I can feel the tears,
just like it was yesterday
although it has been years.

What if I removed the rose?
I may no longer mourn -
though, being realistic,
each garden has a thorn.

How Do I Feel Loved?

"So, how do you feel loved?" you asked.
"I'd love to hear you share.
What are the things that warm your heart?
That let you know I care?"

Your questions took me by surprise;
I felt my cheeks turn pink.
I couldn't answer right away;
I had to stop and think.

I thought of all the gifts you gave,
the time spent having fun,
stimulating conversations
and all the things we'd done.

Then I remembered other times
when stuff got in the way -
fears, defenses, disconnections...
so what was I to say?

My mind tripped over memories
while you watched and waited.
I saw the questions in your eyes
as I hesitated.

I took a breath and smiled at you;
I reached out for your hand.
The answers might not satisfy...
I hoped you'd understand.

"I feel it as we talk and share
and in the things we do,
but most of all I feel so loved
when you let me love you."

Resilience

This mind's been seared with memories
that cannot be erased.
These eyes have cried the stinging tears
that flow when hurts are faced.
These ears have heard too many things
that injured and appalled.
These lips have spoken words aloud
that could not be recalled.
This heart has broken into bits
when loving has caused pain.
This soul has felt a woundedness
when life's been inhumane.

And yet despite these tests and trials,
this person perseveres -
not broken by the storms of life
by hardships, doubts or fears.

How can the mind know loving thoughts
that bring a sense of peace?
And how can eyes release the tears
from having joy increase?
What ears can hear the finest words
that nourish and enrich?
Or lips deliver love and grace
in perfect tone and pitch?
Whose heart can swell and overflow
when feeling full and right?
Or soul be whole and satisfied
throughout the day and night?

If not for life's adversities
    and facing up to fears,
        could we embrace resilience
            to take us through the years?

The Question

What if I made a date with you
for going out to dine
and as we talked and laughed throughout
I knew I'd make you mine?

What if I held your hand real tight
as we went out and walked
and I was kind and warm and fun
and listened while you talked?

What if I reached into the sky
and did a tender thing
like plucked a perfect star for you
and said it was a ring?

What if I got on bended knee
and looked into your eyes
and asked if you would marry me
and smiled at your surprise?

What if you answered yes to me
and you became my wife
and we set out with hopeful plans
to live a happy life?

What if we had a lengthy time
together through the years
of ups and downs and all-arounds
with laughter and with tears?

What if we reached our ending days
and thought about what's passed
would you go through it all again -
say yes to what I asked?

The Answer

I do recall those memories...
the date and everything -
your sweet proposal in the park
with this engagement ring.

I do remember saying yes
with heartfelt happy tears
and setting out with hopeful plans
for many joyous years.

I do look back upon our lives
and think about the past -
the highs, the lows and in-betweens -
it's all gone by so fast.

I do sense time is shorter now
and I feel very blessed -
indeed I feel my gratitude
cannot be well expressed.

I do know I would answer yes -
yes, we were meant to be;
yes, I'd go through it all again;
yes, for eternity.

Sweet Jesus

Uttered softly under my breath,
exclaimed in grateful triumph,
sobbed into tear-soaked hands,
whispered in heartfelt prayer,
groaned in downright disbelief,
laughed in skeptical humour,
yelled in furious frustration...

... sitting, standing, lying or kneeling,
... privately, publicly, silently or aloud
... in response, in reaction, in reply
to all that is holy or not.

Were I to be allotted a language
comprised of only two words,
these would suffice.
Sweet Jesus, it would seem,
is the language of my soul.

Storyteller

I remember, long ago...
one fine warm autumn day,
I drove out to a local park
not very far away.
My plan was to go walking
and have some time alone;
I started down a winding trail
that wasn't too well known.

I walked along quite quickly
enjoying the fresh air
and as I came around a bend
I saw an old man there.
On a rustic bench he sat
beneath majestic trees,
bright sunlight glinting off grey hair,
a cane across his knees.

Looking up invitingly,
he motioned at the view
remarking on the things he saw
so I sat down there, too.
We exchanged some pleasantries;
he continued talking.
I found him so engaging that
I abandoned walking.

He started reminiscing
and telling of a time
about when he was near my age,
a young man in his prime.
As he shared his memories,
my mind could see each scene.
There were so many things he'd done
and places he had been!

And when each story finished
I thought it was his last
but then he'd find another one
to share about his past.
He spoke of joys and sorrows,
achievements he had earned,
life lessons that had come along,
and all the things he'd learned.

He told me of much hardship
of losses, grief and strife,
the wisdom gained from living long,
and coping with his life.
Yet, even though he'd suffered,
he had a charming way
of relating all the stories
and things he had to say.

Eventually he tired
and looked up with a smile.
He said, "It's been good meeting you.
We've been here quite a while.
I must be getting home now.
You've been so very kind
by sitting here and listening
to all that's on my mind."

With a twinkle in his eyes,
as we got up to stand,
he said he'd be back here again
and warmly shook my hand.
I said it was a pleasure,
that I'd enjoyed our talk,
perhaps I would see him again
when I was on a walk.

Until I was much older
I didn't realize
how meaningful these times can be
but now I'm old and wise.
So when you go out walking
and see me waiting there
sit down and spend some time with me
I have more tales to share.

The Cabin

The little log cabin
amongst all the trees;
the splashing of water,
the cool of the breeze.

The flocks of migrators,
the ducks on the lake,
the evergreens swaying,
the falling snowflake.

The little ones playing,
the dogs running by;
so happy the scene
a tear in my eye.

Voicing Questions

I haven't figured out
  how the world works,
though I've tried -

why annoying mosquitoes
  leave some people alone yet
are relentlessly attracted to me,

why unhealthy foods
  can taste so good when they
are so bad for us,

why so many people are given
  kind and generous natures
and too many are not,

why power and influence cause
  countless leaders to create peace and
some to make war,

why there are people that seem to
  lead easy lives while others
have so many hardships,

why we are born
  and what we're here to do
before we die,

why I have a desire
  to voice these questions
that some wish to avoid.

The Optimist

I've made mountains into molehills,
turned lemons into lemonade
and focus on the positive
and happy memories I've made.

I've had my share of tragedy
and an ocean full of sorrow
yet I can go to sleep each night
with a smile about tomorrow.

At times I do have doubts and fears
and things can make me feel dismayed
but I just turn to sunny thoughts
so there's no rain on my parade.

Though life has knocked me down at times
and suffering has caused some pain,
there's so much to be thankful for
I get myself back up again.

I don't know why hard things happen -
can't figure out what's going on.
I just know that the sun comes up
and there's promise in every dawn.

October Carving

To be able to reach down deep inside,
carve out all the slimy mush of life
and just set it aside
leaving a soft, clean space -
a space where light can shine....

To be able to share that light
through eyes wide open
completely present to those who come near
then depart with a smile
and the reward of sustenance....

To be able to create something...
... something that is significant,
brings joy to a child,
brightens up the world,
even if just for one night....

To be able to participate...
... to celebrate a season
with gratitude and thanksgiving,
with joy and generosity
leaves beautiful colourful memories.

Thank You

Sometimes help comes along
and you didn't really know
you needed it -
or you thought you wanted it
for a certain thing
and you ended up being helped
in an entirely different way.

And when you realize the impact,
it's stunning!
Love and appreciation
explode in your heart
letting light and clarity enter -
and you see the world differently
and feel forever changed.

And it's so beautiful
it takes your breath away
and fills your eyes with tears...
and you feel inadequate
to express all of this in words
because all you can say is
thank you.

Elusive

I might catch a glimpse of it
out of the corner of my eye
only to discover that I was just imagining things.

Sometimes a whiff of its fragrance
might linger in the room -
though it can't be found by sniffing around.

At times I'm sure I hear it call my name
yet I know searching
will only cause it to quietly go into hiding again.

And then there is the flavour -
oh, the unrequited sweetness of it...
when a few pieces aren't enough to satisfy.

My fingers itch with anticipation
of stroking and smoothing its various parts -
if I could just capture it.

My heart remembers with yearning
the delight of passion and depth of sharing
whenever we finally come together.

Beautiful, stirring and satiating -
it causes a craving in my soul.
Sometimes a poem can be so elusive.

Once Upon a Dream

I dreamed I wrote a poem.
I watched myself write it -
working away at my desk,
pausing to stare off into space,
scribbling down words,
tapping my fingertips against the desktop,
writing, editing, finalizing....

When finished, I read it aloud
theatrically, with great gusto,
and was ever so enthusiastic
about my dazzling new work of art.
I shared it with others,
got rave reviews,
and basked in feelings of accomplishment.

Though I have tried,
I can't remember it -
can't bring it back to mind
to write it down now.
All I can do
is write about
dreaming about
writing a poem.

Sophie

This is the story of my dog -
of how she came to live with me
and make my home a brighter place
so full of all her canine glee.

I got a call one Saturday
to help a friend out with a chore;
She'd taken in a little dog
and couldn't keep it anymore.
She asked if I could go with her
to take her dog and give it up.
We set off for a rescue place
and there I saw a special pup.

A skinny little thing she was -
this little pup they'd just got in...
a stray they'd picked up east of here
so cute and fluffy, black as sin.
We didn't want another dog;
I feared what Chris would say to me.
I could not leave this sweet pup there.
I filled out forms and paid the fee.

Without this dog that I brought home,
our lives would just not be the same.
She's happy, smart and full of joy -
and Chris gave her a lovely name.

It is Christmas

Each time we share a heartfelt hug
or hold another's hand,
each time we think of those we love
so far across the land...

Each time we gather with our friends,
glad not to be apart,
share laughter 'til our bellies ache,
give from a grateful heart...

Each time we say a special thanks
for gifts that we receive,
appreciate all that we have
and know what we believe...

Each time we choose to share our selves,
to see another's worth,
to be a voice of love and joy
and hope upon this earth...

... it is Christmas.

Happy New Year!

The eve of a new year is here,
the calendar page will be turned.
I've pondered the days, weeks and months
and thought about all that's been learned.

Through three hundred sixty-five days
the things that have mattered so much
of course are what money can't buy -
like people and good times and such.

Just being with those who are dear,
each moment of health, peace and love,
and work that's rich and rewarding
are blessings sent down from above.

The time spent with family and friends
brought joy that cannot be measured.
Those memories are tucked in my heart,
so very precious and treasured.

Of course there were other moments -
those moments we cannot explain;
the trials of life, the ups and downs,
the losses and things that cause pain.

I've spent the day reminiscing,
remembering smiles and some tears,
and now it's time to look forward -
so let's raise a glass and say 'Cheers!'

For Specific People

Happy Birthday My Friend!

When I think of you my friend,
I feel so richly blessed.
You add so much to my life
and you bring out my best.

When a phone call brings your voice
my heart begins to smile -
even if we've just had lunch
or if it's been a while.

You're a very special gal
who's loved by all your friends
for your warm and caring ways
and love that never ends.

You're so fun to spend time with;
we don't need things to do.
We have such great times talking
and get the giggles, too!

We can freely share our tears
and hear each other's pain -
and you remind me often
there's sunshine after rain.

When I think of you my friend
I feel so richly blessed.
I'm grateful that I know you -
you stand out from the rest!

For the birthday of a friend

A Steamy Night

You come with joy and eagerness;
you come in the night when it's dark.
You get in your car and you drive -
then look for a good place to park.

You walk up the path and are here.
It's when you arrive I can see
you've gotten dressed with special care
in clothes that are meant just for me.

It's cold outside and I'm waiting
to gather you into my heat,
to soothe all your stresses away
and caress you from head to feet.

I know you've been yearning for me
as I have been waiting for you
and you've been anticipating
the soothing only I can do.

You greet me with your smiling eyes,
throw back the cover with a sigh
and slide yourself into my curves,
all tension going by-the-by.

You fit your body next to mine
while gently I caress your skin
and time goes by unnoticed now
as all our focus is within.

We have a rich and special time
and finally you have to go -
you have to leave my warm embrace
but you'll come back again we know.

You dress yourself for going home
and give your tingling skin a rub.
You think how very blessed you are
to spend time in a friend's hot tub!

For a friend in honour of spending many enjoyable evenings sharing great conversation over glasses of wine in her luscious hot tub.

Dear Jim

When we remember you, dear Jim,
we think of you so fit and trim
when you were with us every day -
before disease took you away.

We think of how you liked to joke,
of twinkling eyes and how you spoke,
your liveliness, your joy for life,
your love for God and for your wife.

You were a part of many things
enjoying all that church life brings
but then your life came to an end.
It's something hard to comprehend.

We know you're in a better place
experiencing God's wondrous grace
but still we're sad and so we grieve
'cause we did not want you to leave.

In memory of a friend

Memories

Sunbeams and buttons
and trying on frames,
coffee and gardens
and silly kids' games,
poems, cards and reading,
each telephone call,
Tuesdays and swinging -
I savoured them all.

Bridges and tree stumps,
and laughter and tears,
the weekends away
and sharing of fears,
great holiday meals
and drives in the fall,
photos and emails -
I savoured them all.

Sweet memories made
in time gone too swift
I value them all
for each was a gift.

In memory of times shared with a friend

In the room where we meet....

She is there when we arrive,
transforming the room with opportunities for growth
radiating patience, kindness, good humour....

We join a circle burdened with issues,
with the over-ripe scent of fruitless attempts
to ignore dead elephants and lonely children,
vulnerable, fearful, courageous....

Words paint pictures,
laughter and tears provide release,
glimmers of hope land on us.

She gently reaches into a swirling chaos of confusion
providing clarity, she envelops us with acceptance
and nurtures us with warmth.
She is there when we arrive.

In the room where we meet....

For a friend who runs therapy groups

Family

My family might not realize,
they somehow may not see,
just how important each one is
and what they mean to me.

Connection with them gives me strength
when trials of life appear;
through thick and thin, through ups and downs
they help me persevere.

They make the good times richer, too -
with laughter, jokes, good cheer...
and time shared with them warms my heart;
I'm blessed to have them near!

For my family

Bedtime Prayer

Before I close my eyes tonight
I offer up this prayer -
requests I'm making for myself
and those for whom I care.

I wish us soft and peaceful dreams
where things will go our way
and hope we rise from sleeping well
refreshed to face the day.

No matter how the weather is
may sunshine fill each soul
and warmth from everyone we meet
sustain and keep us whole.

May gratitude enrich our day,
compassion be our guide
and loving kindness overflow
from somewhere deep inside.

Let us have hearts filled up with song,
with light and joy and peace
and may tomorrow bring the things
that help our hope increase.

And when the day comes to a close
may we look back and see
the many blessings that have been
bestowed on you and me.

For my family and friends

Various Forms

In my writing group, we learn about and explore **various forms** of poetry. This section contains some of my favourites with descriptions of each form. You might like to try them out.

If you enjoy the various forms of poetry in this section, there are many more forms to be found on numerous excellent websites. I particularly enjoy the websites that provide poetry lesson outlines for children. As well as keeping things simple and easy to understand, they have very good descriptions and examples.

Haiku

Haiku poetry is an ancient form of Japanese verse. A traditional haiku contains a total of 17 syllables on 3 lines, arranged in a pattern of 5-7-5. Two simple subjects are placed in juxtaposition and sometimes separated by punctuation. These poems contain a seasonal reference, are about nature or the natural world, and usually don't have a title.

Modern Japanese haiku are less likely to follow the traditional pattern of 17 syllables or to have nature as their subject, but do use juxtaposition. They may be more about observed everyday objects or occurrences than about nature.

Vacation Haiku

I love Florida!
Escaping from cold winters
saves my sanity.

Hopeful Haiku

Locked up inside for too long,
words come tumbling out
to land upon the paper.

Diamante

A diamante (dee-uh-MAHN-tay) is a non-rhyming seven-line poem. 'Diamante' is Italian for 'diamond'. The first and last lines are the shortest, with longer lines in the middle, which gives these poems a diamond shape. There are two types of diamantes - *synonym* diamantes and *antonym* diamantes.

The diamante is a fairly recent form of poetry. It was created by American poet Iris McClellan Tiedt in 1969.

The rules for a diamante:

1. Diamantes are seven lines long.
2. The first and last lines have just one word.
3. The second and sixth lines have two words.
   The third and fifth lines have three words.
   And the fourth line has four words.
4. Words on lines 1, 4, and 7 are nouns.
   Words on lines 2 and 6 are adjectives.
   Words on lines 3 and 5 are verbs.

In a synonym diamante, the nouns on lines 1 and 7 are words that mean basically the same thing. In an antonym diamante, these two nouns are opposites.

Love and Hate

Friend
pleasurable, enjoyable
loving, laughing, listening
companion, pal – foe, adversary
hating, fighting, opposing
hostile, loathsome
Enemy

Life

Birth
miraculous, laborious
arriving, entering, beginning
life, existence – passage, transition
leaving, exiting, ending
sad, mournful
Death

Nonet

A nonet consists of nine lines which are written in the following structure.

line 1 - 9 syllables
line 2 - 8 syllables
line 3 - 7 syllables
line 4 - 6 syllables
line 5 - 5 syllables
line 6 - 4 syllables
line 7 - 3 syllables
line 8 - 2 syllables
line 9 - 1 syllable

This form of poem can be on any subject and rhyming is optional.

Thanksgiving

It's with amazement that I give thanks
for the joy of co-creating
a delightful oasis
in my cozy backyard -
a place of soothing
serenity.
This garden
feeds my
soul.

Autumn

Autumn is my favourite season.
It's filled with amazing colour,
fresh crisp air, long shadows and
preparing the garden,
as well as myself,
to settle in
for a long
winter
sleep.

Pantoum

The pantoum dates back to the fifteenth century in Malaysia. It was made up of two rhyming couplets that were sung or recited aloud and could go on as long as the poet wished.

Pantoums may vary in their structure and patterns of repetition. A common version is written in stanzas of four lines. It requires a smooth rhythm and flow of language and the rhyming is generally a-b-a-b. The first stanza contains the first four original lines. After that, each new stanza will repeat the previous second and fourth lines but in the new positions of the first and third lines respectively. The pantoum can be as long as you wish following that pattern for repeating lines. The last stanza always uses the first and third lines from the original first stanza.

Pantoum for a Beloved Pet

She searches deeply in my eyes.
She rubs her cheek against my hand.
This lovely creature's old and wise.
It seems that she can understand.

She rubs her cheek against my hand.
I try to push my grief away.
It seems that she can understand.
The future holds a certain day.

I try to push my grief away.
I wonder if she feels some fear.
The future holds a certain day.
She seems to know the end is near.

I wonder if she feels some fear.
This lovely creature's old and wise.
She seems to know the end is near.
She searches deeply in my eyes.

In memory of our beloved Charity 2000 - 2014

Slap-dash

Slap-dash is a term I created to describe the type of poem I write when I have left my writing class homework to the last minute. I just quickly throw something peppy together that might elicit a chuckle.

Homework Woes

I'm running on empty
and all through the week
a little more sleep
is all that I seek.

It is Murphy's law
that things will go wrong.
That's been the problem
all through the week long.

There's just too much work
and that's my refrain -
and why my homework
is not done again.

Writer's Block

No flow'ry phrases can I write,
no words to make you think,
no rambling prose so picturesque
to cause the brain to kink.

Sometimes it just comes pouring out
from somewhere deep inside.
At other times the words aren't there -
no matter how I've tried!

So for today I've given up
and this is what you get.
I grabbed a pen and wrote it down
before I could forget.

I didn't want to come without
some homework in my hand
so this is all I brought today.
I knew you'd understand.

Acrostic

An acrostic is a poem, usually in verse, in which the first letter, syllable or word of each line, paragraph or other recurring feature in the text spells out a word, name, phrase or message.

A simple acrostic, called an 'alphabetical acrostic' or Abecedarius, spells out the letters of the alphabet in order. These acrostics can be found in the first four of the five songs that comprise the Book of Lamentations, in the praise of the good wife in Proverbs 31, 10-31, and in Psalms 9, 10, 25, 34, 37, 111, 112, 119 and 145 of the Hebrew Bible.

Acrostics are commonly found in medieval literature where they usually highlighted the name of the poet or his patron or were used as a prayer to a saint. They were also popular during the Renaissance, used in complicated ways to encipher and hide messages.

The Essence of Autumn

Trees abound with vivid hue
Hours of light decrease
Eastern winds are blowing in
Each day I hear the geese
Snow is promising to come
Sunshine's not as warm
Early evenings settle in
Next there might be a storm
Crunchy leaves are underfoot
Each farmer's working hard
Overhead the flocks fly south
Fall chores wait in my yard
All the squirrels are gathering
Up food that will sustain
To keep them through the winter
Until spring comes again
Many months of cold await
Now I prepare to hibernate

Limerick

A Limerick is five lines long with a rhyming scheme of a-a-b-b-a. Often the first line will end with the name of a person or place and the last line is usually humourous. There is a distinctive rhythm ('anapaestic') which looks like this:

da DUM da da DUM da da DUM
da DUM da da DUM da da DUM
da DUM da da DUM
da DUM da da DUM
da DUM da da DUM da da DUM

Find It Quickly!

There was a brown teddy named Morley.
We needed to find him so sorely.
My daughter was crying.
It was very trying
and soon we'd all be doing poorly!

The Way Home

In my dream, it was the middle of the night and all was quiet. I was sleeping lightly, stretched out on my back beside my husband, Chris. I turned my head toward him and became aware of a brightness coming through my eye lids. Opening my eyes, I saw a large ray of light streaming down from the ceiling to the floor in the corner of the room next to Chris' side of the bed. I could see him reflected in the light and marvelled that he continued to sleep soundly despite the brightness beside him.

The ray of light was quite beautiful... thick, rich and golden. I realized I couldn't see through the light so I got out of bed to go study it more closely.

As I sat up and turned to stand, I saw that I had left my body peacefully sleeping behind me. I still appeared to have a body but it seemed a bit lighter and less substantial. There were fewer physical sensations - for instance, I didn't feel the coolness of the autumn night.

I walked around the foot of the bed and stood in front of the light gazing at it with a sense of wonder. Where it landed on the floor, the light was about three feet wide and deep and it narrowed toward the ceiling. I peered into it trying to see Chris' bedside table.

The light was so thick that I couldn't see the bedside table or anything on it, though in my mind, I could picture the clock radio and lamp surrounded by books. Try as I might, I couldn't see a thing... not the floor, the bedside table or the wall behind it.

I studied the light and looked up toward the ceiling. I wondered what might be in the light and smiled at the thought that there might be a staircase or ladder hiding in there. I didn't try to touch the light as I felt uncomfortable with not knowing what my hand might come into contact with.

As I was standing there staring and musing, a voice spoke in my mind in the form of a thought. I was told that this is where I'm to go when I die. My first reaction was to think, *"Okay... that's interesting."* This was immediately followed with a sharp reaction of shock and fear when I thought, *"Oh no, I'm going to die!"* As soon as I began experiencing a panicky feeling about this, I was overcome with a sense of total and utter peace... as though a powerful, loving blanket of reassurance had been wrapped around me. I have never before experienced such peace. It is difficult to describe how infinite and overpowering it felt - and there could be no other possible response to it except complete surrender.

Peaceful and accepting, I turned away from the light and retraced my steps around the foot of the bed. As I came beside my sleeping body and saw it lying there, I felt a warm and caring love for it. I wondered if I would have trouble entering back into my body and if there was a certain way I should do so. No answers came to my mind so I decided to just lie down and see what happened. I turned my back, reclined, and slipped into my body with a natural ease. I settled gently back to sleep.

Soon after, I woke from the dream with a feeling of fear and thinking, *"Oh no! Who's going to die?"* Now wide awake, I immediately jumped to the conclusion that Chris was going to die. Then I remembered that it was *me* who was going to die! The next instant, as soon as panic began to rise, I was blanketed by a warm feeling of peace soothing every nerve and cell in my body. *"Yes... that's right... everything is going to be okay...."* was my last thought before waking to a bright new day.

* * *

Often in the days and weeks that followed this dream of a couple of years ago, I pondered the state of my life. I asked myself if I was ready to die and if I had any unfinished business that needed attending to. I wondered how long I might have left here on this earth and if there was anything in particular that I would like to be doing with my remaining time. As time went on, these thoughts subsided. There was no feeling of urgency, no sense that I would be going up into the light anytime soon. On hearing about this dream, a friend suggested to me that perhaps I was just given the knowledge of what would happen when the time came. I liked that thought.

I came to view this dream as a gift. It caused me to be more aware of how I'd like to live during whatever remaining time is allotted to me. It made me think about the things I like to do, the people I like spending time with and how I'd like to be in this life.

Whenever I think about this dream, I am reminded that I know where I am to go when my earthly life comes to an end. I also know that I will be okay, even if I am somewhere other than in my bedroom when that happens. There will be a beam of light somewhere nearby. I know I will never feel lost... I know the way home. I smile as these memories bring back that wonderful sense of peace again.

Acknowledgements

I want to acknowledge, with special thanks, the many individuals who have worked with me in putting this book together. I am so very grateful for all of their encouragement, support and assistance.

Marcia Taylor helped to initiate this project. Her wonderful sense of humour, outstanding cheerleader qualities and refreshingly honest feedback made it a very enjoyable process.

Kathleen McGovern provided exceptional skills in patiently editing and proofreading. Through many revisions, she gently encouraged me and made many wonderful suggestions that improved the quality of the initial manuscript. Kate, Lin, Verna, Marcia and Beth were very generous with their time and talents during the final proofing process. Their thoughts and ideas were invaluable.

The members of my Friday morning writing group, under the fearless leadership of Beth Beasley, attentively listened with appreciation and gave great feedback. Without their warmth, kindness, and camaraderie, writing wouldn't be nearly so fun and rewarding.

I am blessed to have many amazing friends. Some of them have been involved in this project by happily supporting, listening and responding with enthusiasm. Without them, I can't imagine being able to continue to grow. In no particular order Wendy, Barb, Jackie, Lin, Linda, Krista, Debbie, Joyce, Faith, Pat and Verna... you are so loved and appreciated.

About the Author

Terri Skuce grew up in beautiful Vancouver, British Columbia where she had the opportunity to be influenced by the majesty of nature, the diversity of people and a variety of unique life experiences. She began writing poems at a very young age. As soon as she could spell 'there's a mouse in the house,' she was crafting verses. As a preteen, schoolmates accused her of copying her poems from books.

Over the years, Terri continued writing poems for school assignments and personal self-expression. Most of this writing did not survive many moves and episodes of de-cluttering. One of these moves brought her to Ottawa, Ontario where she currently resides.

In her professional life, Terri's writing primarily consists of letters, reports, procedures, presentations and other business documents. As well, for a time, she worked as a weekly news columnist, writing about community happenings for a small local newspaper.

As her family became more independent, Terri returned to her love of expressing herself through her writing. She has been a member of a local writing group for several years.

Terri has been influenced by too many favourite poets to list; however, three that stand out for her are Mary Oliver, Maya Angelou and Rumi.

61668832R00067

Made in the USA
Charleston, SC
25 September 2016